LUCY
Meets a
DRAGON

Written by Susan Reid
Illustrated by Greg Rogers

Lucy and her father were moving into a new house.

Lucy was having great fun exploring the rooms and looking in all the cupboards.

In the cupboard under the stairs, Lucy found a huge trunk. She wondered what was inside, but it was too dark to see.

"Dad, come and look! I've found something!" Lucy called excitedly.

Together they pushed and pulled the trunk into the light.

Lucy's father lifted the lid.

Out spilled silk that was purple and blue and green and yellow. It was just like a rainbow.

Lucy reached into the trunk and threw folds of material into the air.

"Oh, how beautiful!" she said.

4

Then Lucy gasped
and froze with horror.

"What is it?"
asked her father.

"Eyes," whispered Lucy.
"Two big black eyes!"

5

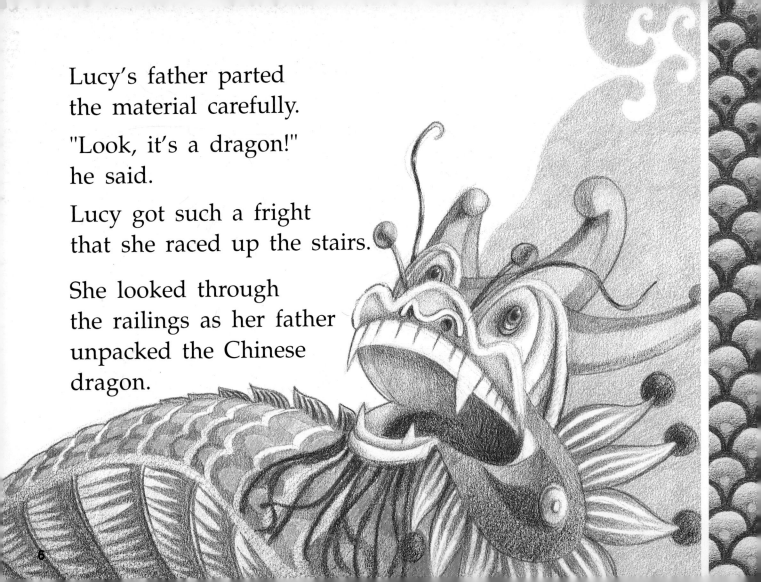

Lucy's father parted
the material carefully.

"Look, it's a dragon!"
he said.

Lucy got such a fright
that she raced up the stairs.

She looked through
the railings as her father
unpacked the Chinese
dragon.

"Don't be silly, Lucy. It can't hurt you. It can decorate the dining room until we find the owners."

7

That night when Lucy
was getting ready for bed,
she thought she heard
strange noises downstairs.

Feeling very curious, she crept half way down the stairs and listened more closely.

"Sniffs," she said to herself. "It sounds like sniffs and snuffles."

Lucy tip-toed to the door
of the dining room
and peeped in.

The dragon was wiping
his eyes on the curtains.
With a deafening roar,
he blew his nose on them
as well.

"Stop it!" cried Lucy,
much to her own surprise.
"You'll ruin our curtains."

The dragon was startled.

"But I'm so unhappy!"
he wailed. "My owners have
left me behind. I'm lonely —
and I'm afraid of the dark!"

Then he whispered,
"Could you please stay
and keep me company?"

Lucy stared in amazement.

"But you look so fierce,"
she said. "I didn't think
anything would frighten you."

"I can't help the way I look,"
sniffed the dragon.

as golden
down the
and dripped
of his nose.

paint is
sobbed.

eyes
cloth.

"I'll never be able to lead
a parade again looking
like this," he said.

Lucy looked into the dragon's big, sad eyes and thought.

"I have an idea," she said. Then she lifted the dragon into her arms.

"I hope I'm not hurting you, Mr. Dragon," she panted as she pulled him up the stairs.

"Will it help if I wriggle
a bit?" said the dragon.
"That's the worst part about
not having legs. I have to
wriggle like a worm
or slither like a snake
to get anywhere.
But when I've got legs
I can dance and prance
all day."

Lucy took the dragon to her room. When he caught sight of his smudged face in the mirror he closed his eyes and moaned.

"Shhh," whispered Lucy, as she searched in her toybox. "I'm sure that I can fix your paintwork if you'll just keep still."

Lucy set to work while the dragon chatted excitedly about fireworks, music, and parades. He had led a very exciting life.

"You must come with me to a parade, Lucy. They're so exciting!" he said.

Then he sneezed. "Atchoo!"

"Shhh," whispered Lucy.

"I can't help it," said the dragon. "Your paintbrush is tickling my nose."

Lucy gently painted
the end of the
dragon's nose.

"There! I've finished.
What do you think?"
she asked.

The dragon looked in
the mirror.

"I look fantastic!"
he said happily.

"And I *feel* wonderful,"
he yawned. "I'm much
too excited to sleep."

But very soon the dragon
was snoring.

In the morning, Lucy and her father were carrying the dragon downstairs when the telephone rang.

It was the people who had owned the house before.

"We think we left our dragon behind. Can we come and get him?" they asked.

They were very pleased to see that their dragon was safe and sound.

"He looks even better than we remember!" they said.

Then they said something that made Lucy very happy.

"Perhaps you would like to help carry our dragon in the parade next Saturday."

Lucy nodded with delight, and she was sure that the dragon gave her a wink.

On Saturday, the dragon led the parade down Main Street.

He danced and pranced along the street, sending puffs of smoke toward the laughing crowd.

Peeping out from under the dragon's tail,
Lucy saw his great big smile
and his shining golden curls.

She knew that the dragon
was happy now,
and she felt happy, too!